Order No.NO18798
ISBN 0.7119.1421.4

Exclusive Distributors:
Music Sales Limited
8/9 Frith Street,
London W1V 5TZ, England.
Music Sales Pty Limited
120 Rothschild Avenue,
Rosebery, NSW 2018,
Australia.

Beatles Guitar.

▶▶▶ *Wise Publications*
London/New York/Sydney

Designed by Pearce Marchbank Studio
Photographs courtesy of
London Features International
Pictorial Press
EMI Records

Printed in the United Kingdom by
Redwood Books, Trowbridge, Wiltshire

14-95

Introduction.

You've all heard of Lennon and McCartney, the songwriting duo, but what about Lennon and Harrison – the guitar duo? Well, that's what you are going to discover in the Beatles Guitar book.

This book is a special work containing a selection of Beatles' tunes arranged exclusively for the guitar. It is designed to provide an accurate look into the lead and rhythm guitar styles of George Harrison and John Lennon.

Although the arrangements in this book are written to embody the essence and style of the guitar works of Lennon and Harrison, the arrangement is not just a transcription of the guitars right off the record. Rather, it uses all of the musical elements: bass, drums, keyboards and guitars, just as The Beatles used them, but all incorporated into one guitar so that you can play the arrangement alone or in a band.

Section I: *Melodic Licks That Signature A Song.*

Section II: *Rhythmic Licks That Signature A Song.*

Section III: *Rhythmic And Melodic Licks That Signature A Song.*

Alphabetical Listing.

Editor's Notes.

The book is divided into three sections:
1. *Melodic Licks That Signature A Song*
2. *Rhythmic Licks That Signature A Song*
3. *Rhythmic And Melodic Licks That Signature A Song*

Section I:

This section includes songs that are most characterised by the use of a melodic signature theme. Songs like 'Day Tripper', 'Ticket To Ride', 'Julia' or 'Lucy In The Sky With Diamonds'.

This does not mean that you have only the lead or bass guitar in the song, but rather that their importance is the driving force behind the tune. The rhythm guitar complements the bass and lead licks in this case.

Section II:

This section contains songs whose signature is the rhythm guitar. In other words, Lennon's rhythm guitar takes prominence over Harrison's guitar and McCartney's bass or keyboards.

Again, you may have some guitar or bass licks, but they take a back seat to the rhythm guitar.

This section is also important and unique in that it affords a guitar player the chance to learn how to play rhythm guitar patterns which incorporate percussive qualities that any good rhythm guitarist should know. Lennon was a brilliant rhythm guitarist and you'll benefit by learning these tunes as arranged.

Section III:

This section contains songs whose signature is both melodic and rhythmic. Let's face it, most songs by The Beatles are a meshing together of melodic and rhythmic elements. Lennon, Harrison and McCartney did not operate in separate little compartments known as rhythm, lead and bass guitar, but rather merged their functions together. In this section we see how most of their songs are a fine balance between rhythmic and melodic essence. Sometimes it's Lennon's effective rhythm guitar behind the verse and chorus, followed by Harrison blending in a nice solo and bridge that goes back into the strong rhythmic verse section, or Lennon trading off with McCartney's bass or Harrison's smaller lick sections.

It's all put together for you in the Beatles Guitar book.

In addition, please note that the guitar part is written in guitar tablature to accommodate musicians who read music, as well as those who do not.

For those who do not read, you can follow the tablature numbers, strums, accents and picking patterns, which you'll learn how to use on the instruction page for tablature (see page 5).

For those who read music, you can follow all of the above, as well as the added musical elements that are included in the tablature line.

All chord changes are shown by the chord frames above the voice line. The voice line gives you the lyrics, melody and which key the song is in.

How To Read Tablature.

1. Tablature is made up of 6 lines, representing the 6 strings of the guitar. The top line represents the first, or highest string on the guitar, while the bottom line represents the sixth, or the lowest string on the guitar. This can be seen in Ex.1.

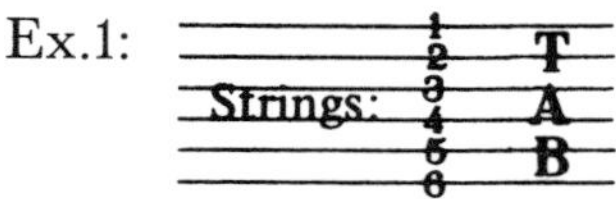

2. The numbers on each line indicate which fret, on that particular string, is to be pressed. For example, if the number 5 is on the 3rd line, this means that the 5th fret on the 3rd string is to be pressed. The number 0 means to play the open string.

⊓ = Down Pick or Down Strum.
V = Up Pick or up Strum.

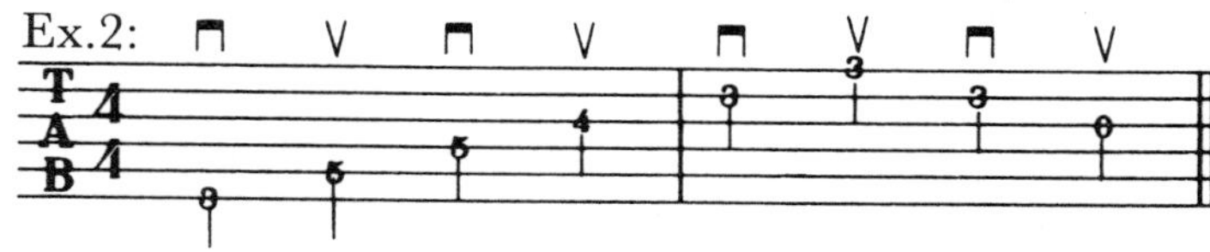

3. A slash (/) is used to indicate strumming. Stemming and beaming indicate rhythm as in ordinary music notation.

B – Strum bass, or lower strings (the 2 or 3 lower strings),
M – Strum middle strings (the 3 or 4 middle strings).
T – Strum treble, or high strings (the 2 or 3 higher strings).
⌐ ┐ (dotted line) – continue previous symbol.

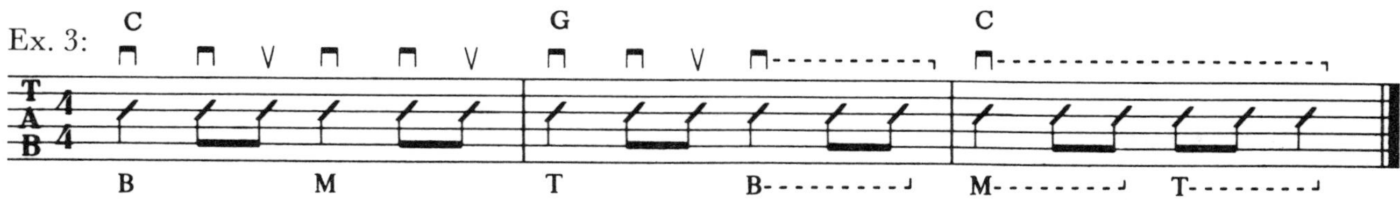

4. (X) The chordal X indicates a muffled sound to be played on a chord. This is achieved by touching lightly (not pressing) the strings of the chord.

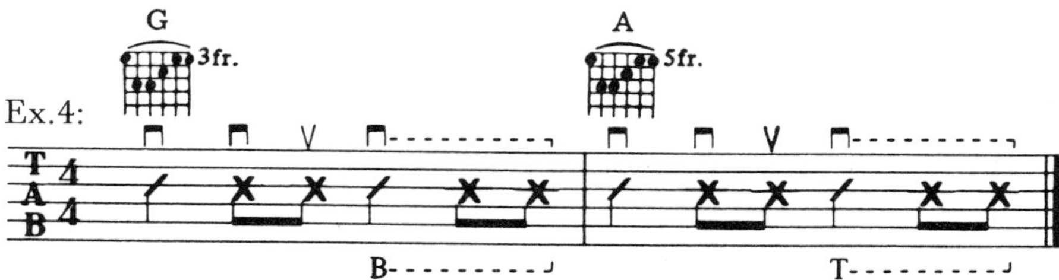

5. (×) The single note × indicates a muffled sound to be played on a single note. The technique is the same as the chordal X.

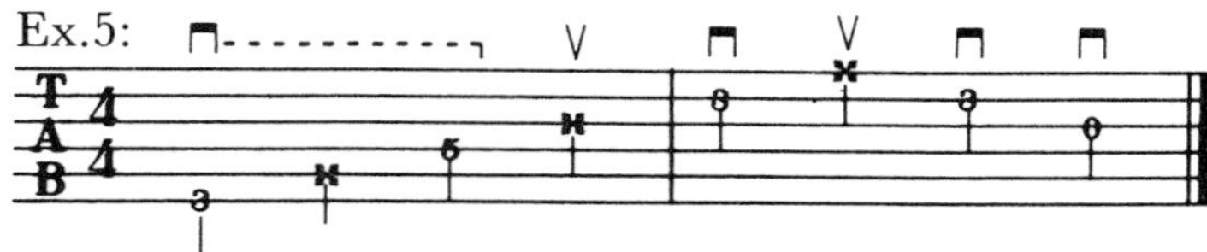

6. Common music symbols, such as the following, are also used with tablature.

> = accent
• = staccato
𝄐 = fermata

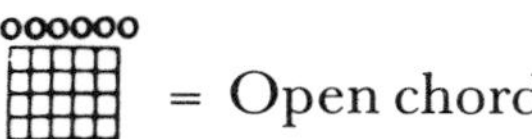

= Open chord

I Feel Fine.

Words & Music by John Lennon & Paul McCartney

Bright rock
D7
C7
Lay down 1st finger, left hand, on both 5th string & nut of the guitar
G
G
1. Ba - by's good to me, you know, she's hap - py as can be, you know, she said so.
2. Ba - by says she's mine, you know, she tells me all the time, you know, she said so.
3. Ba - by says she's mine, you know, she tells me all the time, you know, she said so.
D

* Mixolydian mode, not key of C

C
G
I'm in love with her and I feel fine. (repeat to 2nd lyric)
I'm in love with her and I feel fine. (continue)
I'm in love with her and I feel fine. (continue)
G
3fr.
Bm
C
I'm so glad that she's my lit - tle girl.
D
G
3fr.
Bm
She's so glad she's
C
D
G
tell - ing all the world that her ba - by buys her things,

— you know, — he buys her dia - mond rings —
B
D
— you know, — she said so.
B T
She's in love — with
B
C
To Coda
G
me and I — feel — fine. —
B
B

G
3fr.
D
D.S. al Coda
Coda
G
D
C
G
She's in love with me and I feel fine.
Repeat and fade

You Can't Do That.

Words & Music by John Lennon & Paul McCartney

Moderato

G* G7 C7 G

mf

(1.) I got some - thing to say that might 'cause you pain; If I catch you talk - in' to that boy a - gain, I'm gon - na let you down and leave you flat,

(2.) sec - ond time I've caught you talk - in' to him; do I have to tell you one more time I think it's a sin. I think I'll let you down

(Let you down gon - na let you down and leave you flat.) Be - cause I've

(Background vocals: 2nd and 3rd times)

* Originally recorded in G♭

D7
3fr.
C7
G7
3fr.
told you be - fore: Oh, you can't do that.
T
A
B
1. D7
2. G7
B7
7fr.
Em
7fr.
Well, it's the Ev - 'ry - bod - y's green, 'cause
Am
5fr.
I'm the one who won your love. But if they'd seen you
Am
Bm
D7
3fr.
G7
3fr.
talk - in' that way they'd laugh in my face. So please lis - ten to me if you

wan - na stay mine,_ I can't help my feel - ings, I'll go out of my mind._ I'm gon - na
C7
G
let you down and leave you flat,
(Let you down)_
(gon - na let you down and
D7
3fr.
C7
To Coda
leave you flat)_
Be - cause I've told you be - fore: Oh,_ you can't do
G
G
that._ (Shout): Wow!_
Emphasize top note in each chord to bring out melody in the Solo.
(Solo)
(You)
T
A
B

C7
(can't do that)
(You can't do that)
(You
G7
4fr.
D
5fr.
can't do that)
(You can't do that)
(You
G
D.S. al Coda
can't do that)
Ev - 'ry - bod - y's green,
Coda
G
that.

Day Tripper.

Words & Music by John Lennon & Paul McCartney

Moderate rock
N.C.
N.C.
(Let all notes ring as long as possible)
E7
5fr.
1. Got a good rea - son
2. She's a big teas - er,
3. Tried to please her.

for tak - ing the eas - y way out,
she took me half the way there.
she on - ly played one - night stands.
T
A
B
A7
5fr.
Got a good rea - son for
She's a big teas - er,
Tried to please her,
E7
5fr.
F♯
tak - ing the eas - y way out, now. She was a Day
she took me half the way there, now. She was a Day
she on - ly played one-night stands, now. She was a Day
Trip - per, one - way tick - et, yeah; It took me
Trip - per, one - way tick - et, yeah; It took me
Trip - per, Sun - day driv - er, yeah; It took me

A7
5fr.
G♯7
4fr.
C♯
4fr.
3rd time
so
long
to find out,
and I found
so
long
to find out,
and I found
so
long
to find out,
and I found
T
A
B
B B B B
B
7fr.
Last time to Coda
N.C.
out.
(repeat)
out.
(continue)
out.
(to Coda)
XII pos.
solo
B7
7fr.
full
full
3/4
1st Guitar
muffled note
2nd Guitar

*M/B = Strum Bass & Middle Strings

Ticket To Ride.

Words & Music by John Lennon & Paul McCartney

E7
F♯m
D7
She's got a tick-et to ride,
F♯m
D
F♯m
She's got a tick-et to ri - hi - hide,
She's got a tick-et to ride,
T
A
B
E7
1. A
but she don't care!
2. A
She
I

D7
3fr.
don't know why she's rid - in' so high,
she ought - ta
T
A
B
B B B B B B
E
think twice; she ought - ta do right by me.
Be -
B B B B B B
D7
3fr.
fore she gets to say - in' good - bye
she ought - ta
B B B B B B
E
think twice, she ought - ta do right by me.
1. I
2. She
7 5 5 5 7 10 7 14 12 10 12
B B B B B B B

A
think I'm gon - na be sad,
said that liv - ing with me
I think it's to - day
is bring - in' her down.
yeah!
yeah!
The girl that's driv - ing me mad
For she would nev - er be free
Bm7
E7
is go - ing a - way.
when I was a - round.
Yeah!
Oh,
F♯ m
D7
she's got a tick - et to ride,

F♯ m
D
She's got a tick - et to ri - hi - hide,
F♯ m
E7
She's got a tick - et to ride, but she don't care!
1. A
I
2. A
A
Falsetto
Repeat and fade
(1st time only) My ba - by don't care!
T
A
B

Lady Madonna.

Words & Music by John Lennon & Paul McCartney

Brightly, with a beat

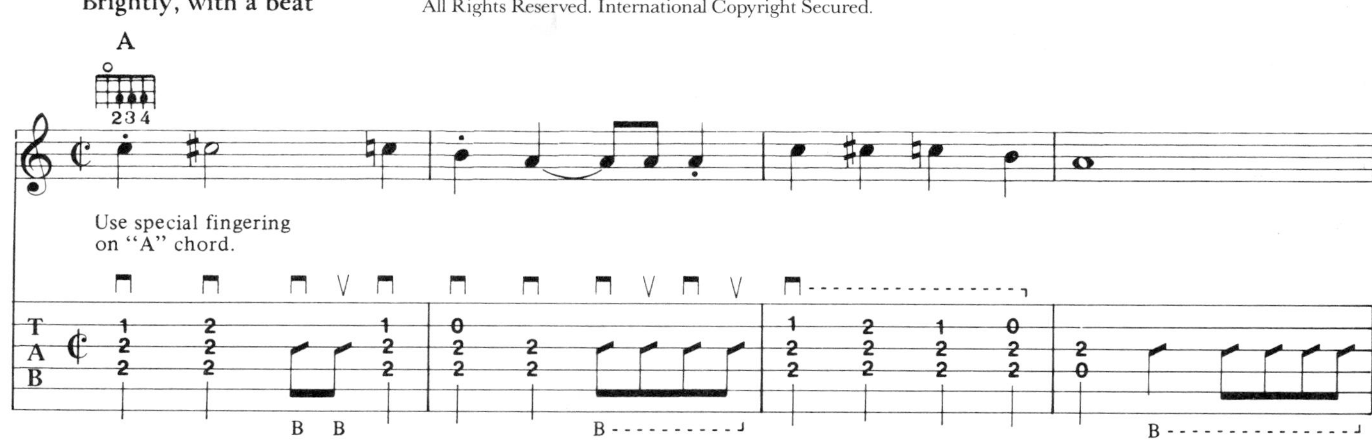

B D B A B B D B

A

Emphasize low note in each strum to bring out bass melody.

D A D

La - dy Ma - don - na, chil - dren at your feet,
La - dy Ma - don - na, ba - by at your breast,
La - dy Ma - don - na, chil - dren at your feet,

A D F 3fr. G *Last time To Coda* A

Won - der how you man - age to make ends meet.
Won - der how you man - age to feed the rest.
Won - der how you man - age to make ends meet. *(to Coda)*

B B

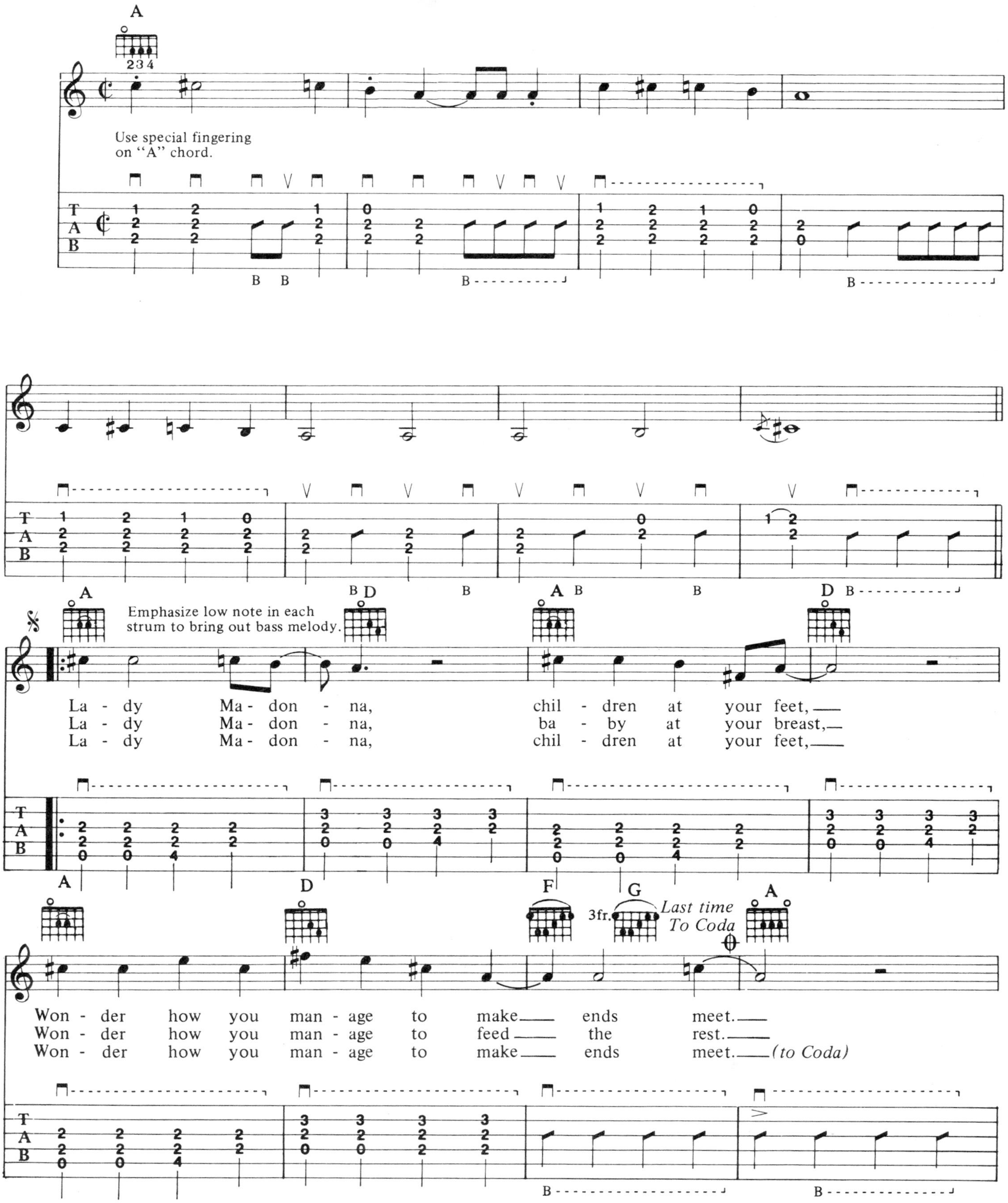

A D A D
Who finds the mon - ey when you pay the rent,
La - dy Ma - don - na ly - ing on the bed,
A D F G 5fr. A
Did you think that mon - ey was heav - en sent?
Lis - ten to the mu - sic play - ing in your head.
Dm G7
Fri - day night ar - rives with - out a suit - case,
Tues - day af - ter - noon is nev - er end - ing,
C Am
Sun - day morn - ing creep - ing like a nun,
Wednes - day morn - ing pa - pers did - n't come,
T
A
B

Dm
G7
Mon - day's child has learned to tie his boot - lace.
Thurs - day night your stock - ings need - ed mend - ing.
B T B T
C
Bm7
D/E
E7
After repeat D.S. al Coda
See how they run!
B T B T
Coda
A
D
Cdim
E7
A
falsetto (opt.)
B
B
A
D
Cdim
E7
A
B

Lucy In The Sky With Diamonds.

Words & Music by John Lennon & Paul McCartney

Moderately
N.C.
mp
A 12fr.
A7/G 10fr.
D/F♯ 9fr.
Dm/F 8fr.
Pic - ture your - self in a boat on a riv - er with
Fol - low her down to a bridge by a foun - tain, where
Pic - ture your - self on a train in a sta - tion with
A/E 12fr.
A7/G 10fr.
D/F♯ 9fr.
F/C 8fr.
tan - ger - ine trees and mar - ma - lade skies.
rock - ing horse peo - ple eat marsh - mal - low pies.
plas - ti - cine por - ters with look - ing glass ties.
(Use pick on bass note. 3 & 4 finger on treble notes for spaced chords)
A/E 12fr.
A7/G 10fr.
D/F♯ 9fr.
Some - bod - y calls you, you an - swer quite
Ev - 'ry - one smiles as you drift past the
Sud - den - ly some - one is there at the

Dm/F 8fr.
A/E 12fr.
A7/G 10fr.
Dmaj7 9fr.
Last time to Coda
slow - ly a girl with ka - lei - do - scope eyes.
flow - ers that grow so in - cred - i - bly high
turn - stile, the girl with ka - lei - do - scope (to Coda)
Dm 10fr.
B♭
Cel - lo - phane
News - pa - per
C9
F6
flow - ers of yel - low and green tow - er - ing
tax - is ap - pear on the shore wait - ing to
B♭
C9
o - ver your head. Look for the
take you a - way (Lay R.H. palm across strings for muffled sound on these two measures) Climb in the

G
(♩. = ♩)
girl with the sun in her eyes and she's
back with your head in the clouds and you're
B
D
G
C
D
10fr.
gone.
gone.
Lu - cy in the sky with dia - monds,
B B B B
B B T B B T
G
C
D
10fr.
G
C
Lu - cy in the sky with dia - monds,
Lu - cy in the sky with
B B B B
B B T B B T
B B B B
D
10fr.
D
After repeat, D.S. al Coda
dia - monds,
Ah
B B T B B T
12 12 12 10 12 12 12

Coda
No chord
eyes.
G
C
D
10fr.
Lu - cy in the sky with dia - monds,
B B T B B
G
C
D
10fr.
G
C
Lu - cy in the sky with dia - monds,
Lu - cy in the sky with
B B T B B
D
10fr.
A
5fr.
Repeat and fade
dia - monds,
Ah.
B B T B B

Michelle.

Words & Music by John Lennon & Paul McCartney

Am
C7/4
F
E7/4
love you, I love you, I love you, that's all I want to say. Un - til I find a way
need to I need to, I need to I need to make you see. Oh, what you mean to
T
A
B
Am
Am-I
E+
Am7
Am6
Fmaj7
1.
E
I will say the on - ly words I know that you'll un - der - stand.
me until I do, I'm hop - ing you will know what I
2.
E
A
Dm7
G
mean. I love you.
F#dim
E
D#dim
E
Am
I want you, I want you, I
C7/4
F
E7/4
want you, I think you know by now, I'll get to you some -

Am
Am-I
E+
Am7
Am6
Fmaj7
how. Un - til I do, I'm tell - ing you, so you'll un - der -
E
A
Dm7
G
F♯dim
stand: Mi - chelle, ma belle, sont des mots qui vont tres bien en -
E
D♯dim
E
Am
E+
Am7
Am6
Fmaj7
semble, tres bien en - semble. And I will say the on - ly words I know that you'll un - der-
E
A
Dm7
G
stand, my Mi - chelle.
F♯dim
E
D♯dim
E
A
Repeat and fade

Good Morning, Good Morning.

Words & Music by John Lennon & Paul McCartney

A
D
5fr.
been?"
Noth - ing to do, it's up to you,
B B B B B
E
E7
A
5fr.
I've got noth - ing to say but
B B B
G
3fr.
To Coda
A
D - I
(use bar on D chord)
"It's O. K. Good morn - ing. good morn - ing, good
B B B B B
1. Guitar Strum-I (four measures)
A
A
G
morn - ing, - a."
(Solo 2nd time)
Go - ing to work, don't want to go,
B B - - - -

A
G
— feel - ing low down, Head-ing for home,— you start to roam,— then you're in
A
D - I
A
D - I
town. Ev - 'ry - bod - y knows— there's noth-ing do -
A
D - I
A
D - I
ing, Ev - 'ry - thing is closed,— it's like a ru - in, Ev - 'ry - one you see— is half a - sleep.
A
D - I
A
— and you're on your own,— you're in the street.—
(Lay left hand across strings for staccato)

2.
A
G
V pos.
VI pos.
P.O. H.O. P.O.
P.O. H.O.
VII pos.
V pos.
VI pos.
P.O.H.O.P.O.P.O.H.O.
P.O.H.O.P.O.
D - I
Peo - ple run - ning 'round, it's five o' - clock. Ev - 'ry - were in town it's get - ting dark,
Ev - 'ry - one you see is full of life, it's time for tea and meet the wife.
D.S. al Coda

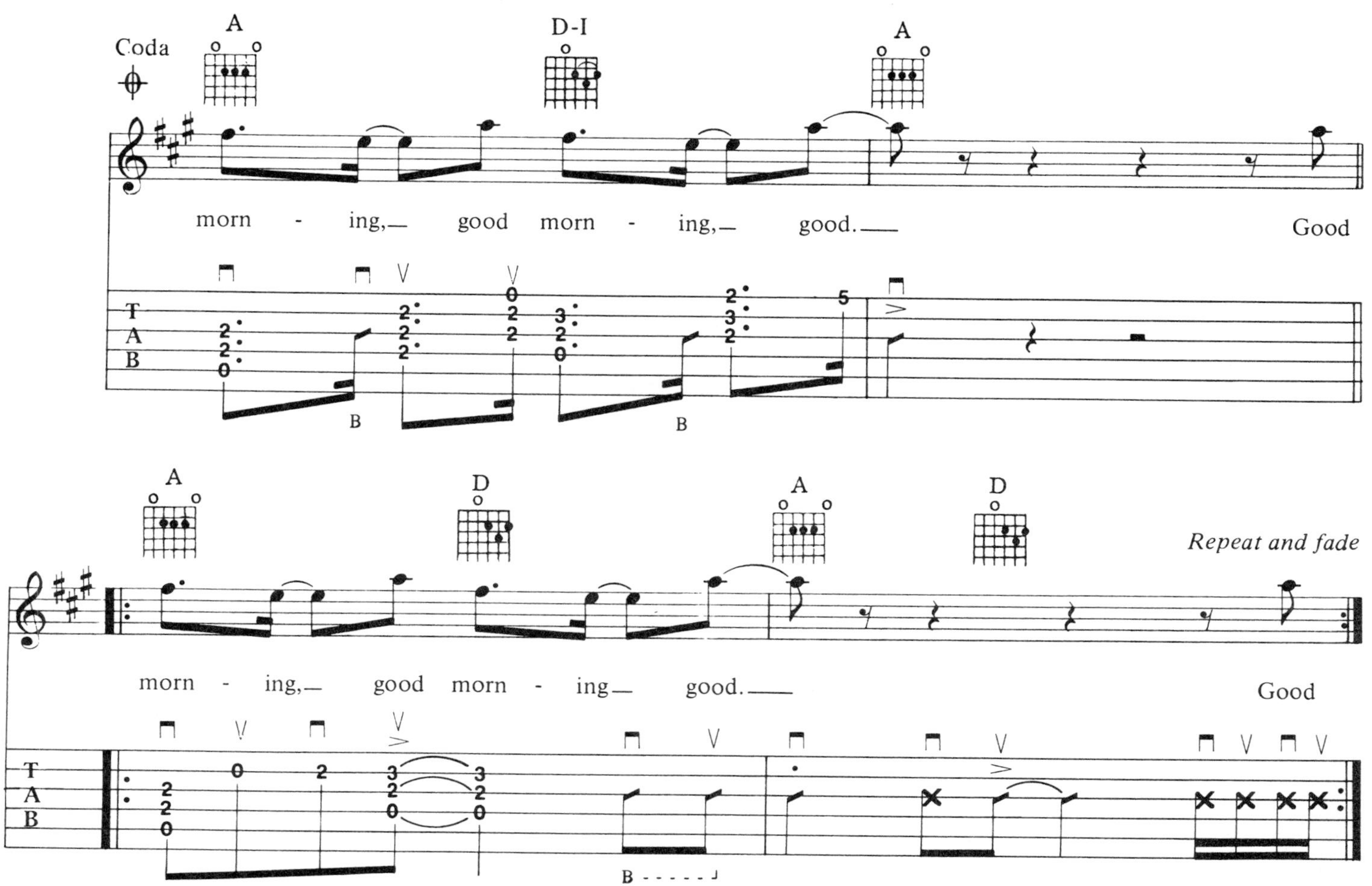

2. After a while you start to smile, now you feel cool.
   Then you decide to take a walk by the old school.
   Nothing has changed, it's still the same,
   I've got nothing to say etc.

3. Somebody needs to know the time, glad that I'm here.
   Watching the skirts, you start to flirt, now you're in gear
   Go to a show, you hope she goes,
   I've got nothing to say etc.

Dear Prudence.

Words & Music by John Lennon & Paul McCartney

D
D/C
Gmaj7/B
Gm(+7)/B♭
Pru - dence,
Pru - dence,
Pru - dence,
greet the brand new day.
see the sun - ny skies.
like a lit - tle child.
To Coda
The
The
The
f
sun is up, the sky is blue, it's beau - ti - ful and so are you. Dear
wind is low, the birds will sing that you are part of ev - 'ry - thing. Dear
clouds will be a dai - sy chain, so let me see you smile a - gain. Dear
C
G
won't you come out to play?
won't you o - pen up your eyes?
won't you let me see you smile?
T
A
B

1.3.
D
D/C
Gmaj7/B
Gm(+7)/B♭
(2.) Dear
(3.) Dear
2. D
Dsus4
D5
Dsus4
D
Dsus4
(Backing) round round round round round
Look a - round, round,
D
Dsus4
D
Dsus4
D
Dsus4
round round round round round
round round round round round round round
Look a - round, round, round,
Look a -
D.S. al Coda 4th time
F
A
5fr.
G
D
D7
Gmaj7/D
Gm(+7)/D
round.
Dear
B
B
B

Coda
D
D/C
Gmaj7/B
Sun is up, the sky is blue, it's beau - ti - ful, and
B B B B
Gm(+7)/B♭
D7/A
Cadd9
G
so are you. Dear Pru - dence, won't you come out to
B B B B
D
D 14fr.
Am7/D 10fr.
D 10fr.
Am7/D 8fr.
play.
(Fading out)
p
B B B
G/D 7fr.
A/D 5fr.
Am7/D
DaddE
ppp

Blackbird.

Words & Music by John Lennon & Paul McCartney

Slowly

G Am7 G G 10fr.

(must be played fingerstyle)

Not to be played off chord positions

Slide up from 3fr. 2nd string

G Am7 G G 10fr.

1. Black - bird sing - ing in the dead of night
2. Black - bird sing - ing in the dead of night

C A7 D7 B7-I Em-I Cm-I

Take these bro - ken wings and learn to fly;
Take these sunk - en eyes and learn to see;

(lift finger pressure for staccato)

Gmaj7 A7-I Am7-I Cm-II G A7 D7

All your life you were on - ly wait - ing for this mo - ment to a -
All your life you were on - ly wait - ing for this mo - ment to be

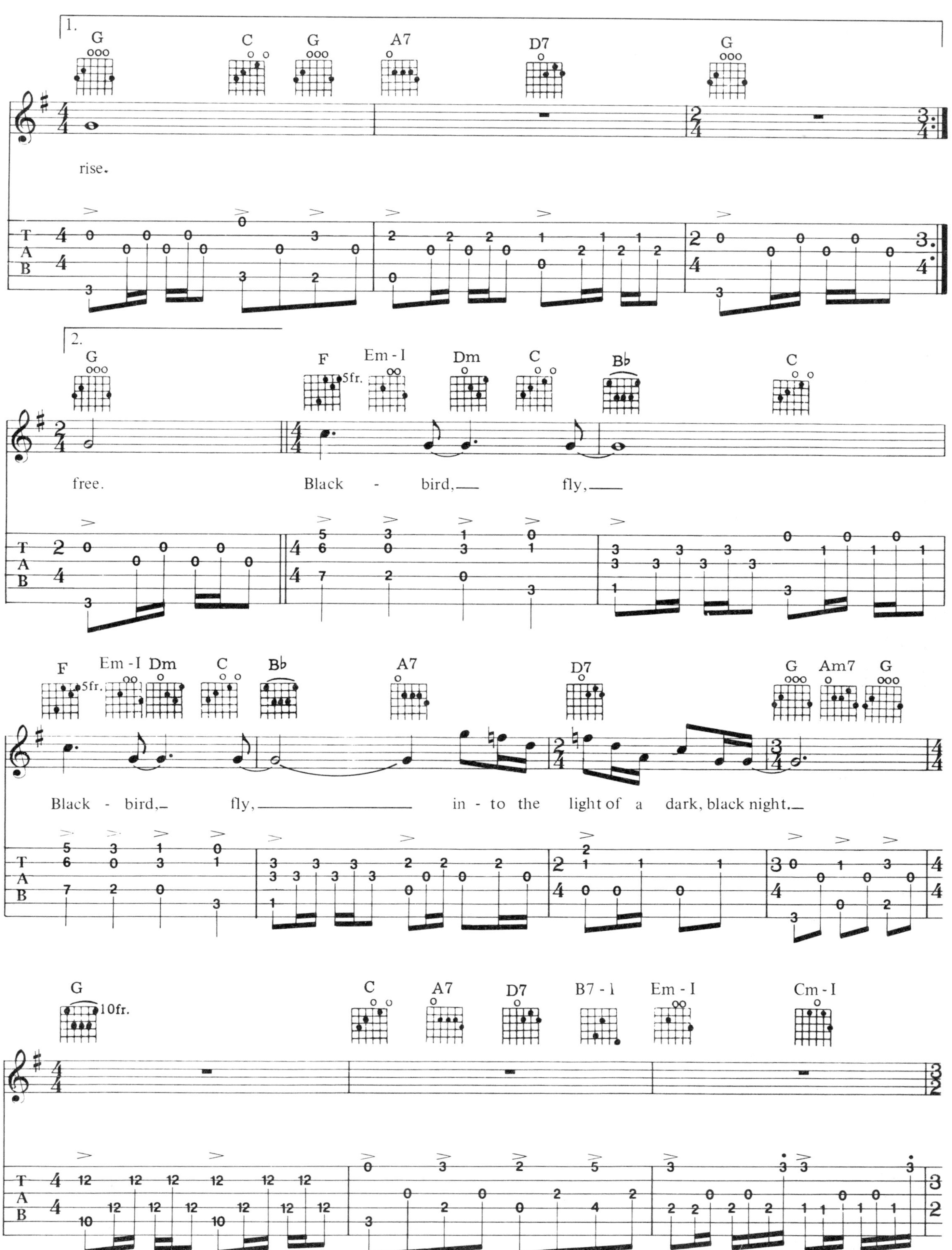
1.
G
C
G
A7
D7
G
rise.
2.
G
F
Em - I
Dm
C
B♭
C
free.
Black - bird,
fly,
F
Em - I
Dm
C
B♭
A7
D7
G
Am7
G
Black - bird,
fly,
in - to the light of a dark, black night.
G
10fr.
C
A7
D7
B7 - I
Em - I
Cm - I

Gmaj7 A7 - I Am7-I Cm-II G A7 D7 G
F 5fr. Em-I Dm C B♭ C F 5fr. Em-I Dm C
Black - bird fly, Black - bird fly,
B♭ A7 D7 G Am7 G
in - to the light of a dark, black - night.
G 10fr.
molto rit.
a tempo

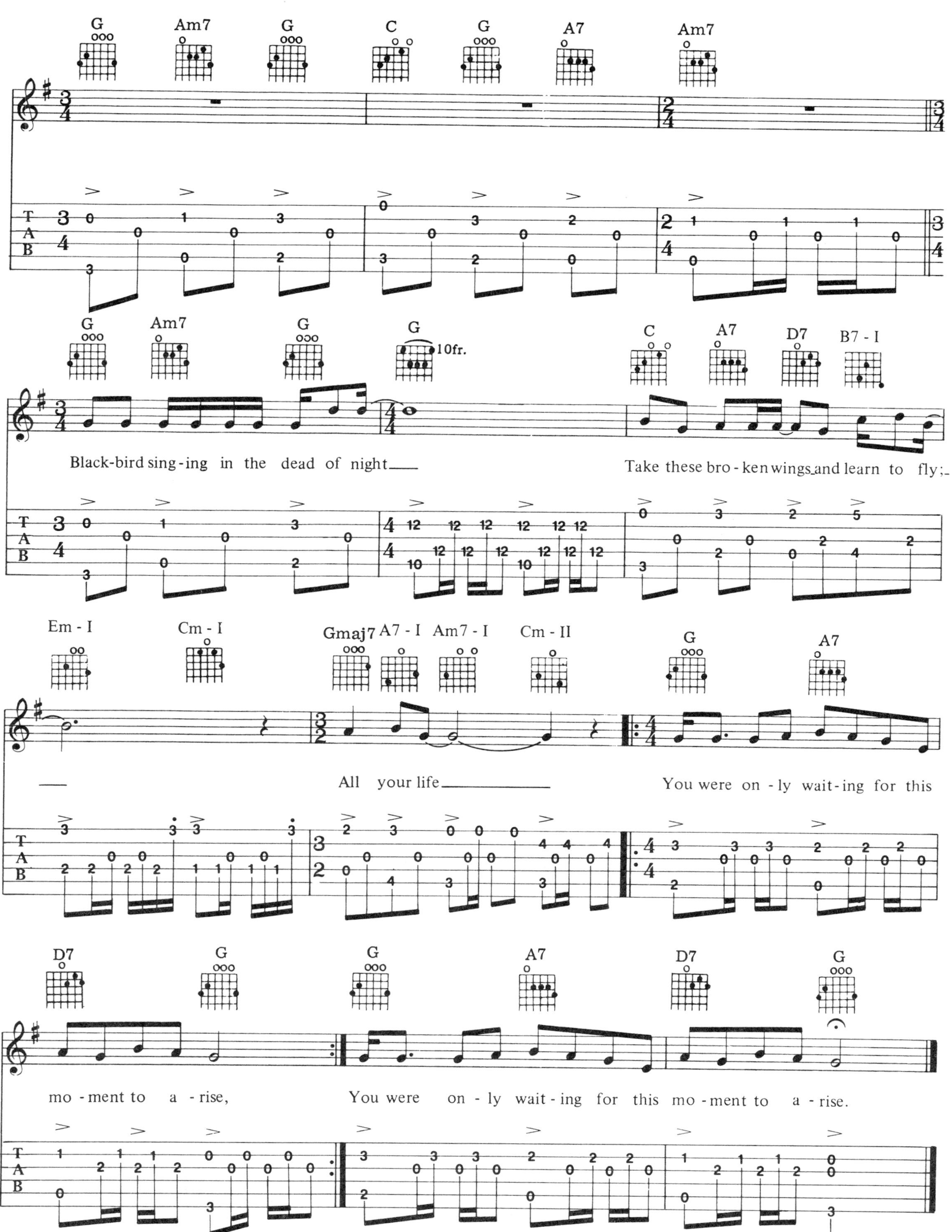
G Am7 G C G A7 Am7
G Am7 G G 10fr. C A7 D7 B7 - I
Black-bird sing-ing in the dead of night
Take these bro - ken wings and learn to fly;
Em - I Cm - I Gmaj7 A7 - I Am7 - I Cm - II G A7
All your life
You were on - ly wait-ing for this
D7 G G A7 D7 G
mo - ment to a - rise,
You were on - ly wait - ing for this mo - ment to a - rise.

Come Together.

Words & Music by John Lennon & Paul McCartney

Moderately slow, with double - time feeling
Tune 6th String to D
Dm
Dm
Here come old flat - top, He come
groov - ing up slow - ly, He got Joo Joo eye - ball, He one
A
7fr.
ho - ly roll - er, He got hair down to his knee.

G
5fr.
Dm
Got to be a jok - er, He just do what he please.
T
A
B
Dm
He wear no shoe - shine, He got toe jam foot - ball, He got
He Bag Pro - duc - tion, He got wal - rus gum - boot, He got
He roll - er coast - er, He got ear - ly warn - ing, He got
mon - key fin - ger, He shoot Co - ca Co - la, He say,
O - no side - board, He one spi - nal crack - er, He got
Mud - dy Wa - ter, He one Mo - jo fil - ter, He say,

A
7fr.
"I know you, you know me."
feet down be - low his knee.
"One and one and one is three."
G
5fr.
One thing I can tell you is you got to be free.
Hold you in his arm - chair, you can feel his dis - ease.
Got to be good look - ing 'cause he so hard to see.
Come to - geth -
Bm
9fr.
A
7fr.
G
5fr.
A
7fr.
To Coda
er, right now, o - ver me
Dm
1.
T
A
B

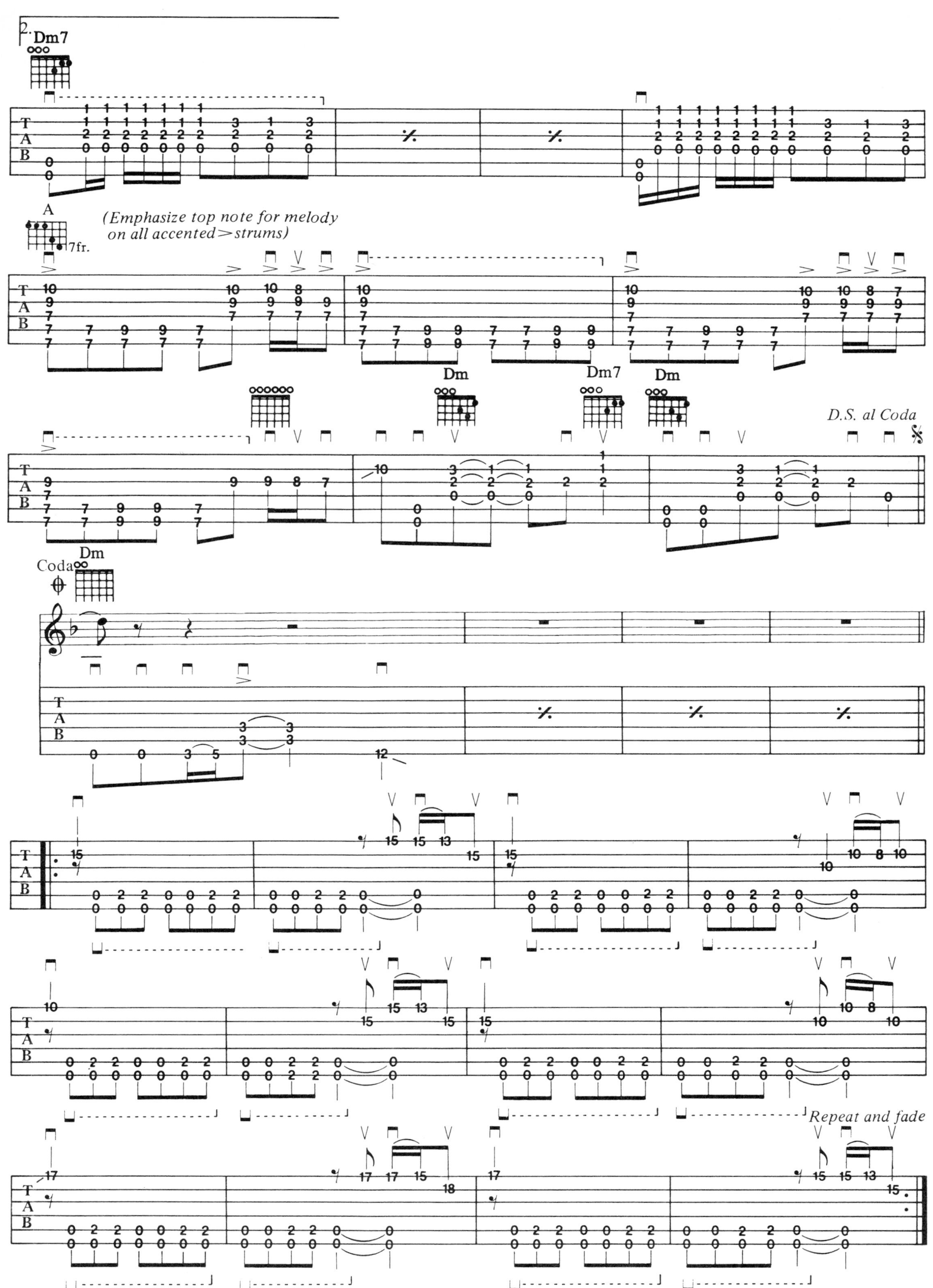

Dm7
A
7fr.
(Emphasize top note for melody on all accented > strums)
Dm
Dm7
Dm
D.S. al Coda
Coda
Dm
Repeat and fade

You Never Give Me Your Money.

Words & Music by John Lennon & Paul McCartney

Slowly
Am
Dm7(add9)
mf
G
C
Fmaj7/C
Bm7
E
Am
Am7
Dm
G
1. You nev - er give me your mon - ey, You on - ly give me your
2. I nev - er give you my num - ber, I on - ly give you my

C
Fmaj7
Dm6
E
fun - ny pa - per, And in the mid - dle of ne - go - ti - a - tions you
sit - u - a - tion, And in the mid - dle of in - ves - ti - ga - tion I
Am
1.
2.C
G7
break down.
break down.
Twice as fast
C
E7
Am
C7
Out of col - lege, mon - ey spent, see no fu - ture, pay no rent,
An - y job - ber got the sack, Mon - day morn - ing, turn - ing back,
F
G7
C
1.
2.
All the mon - ey's gone, no - where to go.
Yel - low lor - ry slow, no - where to go.
(Keep chords down where possible)
But oh,

Original tempo
B♭
F
— that mag - ic feel - ing, no - where to
C
8fr.
B♭
go. Oh, that mag - ic feel - ing
F
C
8fr.
no - where to go, — no - where to go. —
B♭
F
1.2.
C
8fr.
Ah

3.
C
3fr.
C
8fr.
D
5fr.
E♭
G
A
9fr.
Slide & roll off
F♯
6fr.
C7
12fr.
15fr.
B
4fr.
D
E7
D7
One sweet dream
Pick up the bags and get in the lim - ou - sine.
Soon we'll be a - way from here, step on the gas and wipe that tear a - way,

A
B7
Cmaj7
G
A
5fr.
One sweet dream came true to - day,
Cmaj7
G/B
A
Cmaj7
G/B
came true to - day, came true
A
C6
G(add A)
A
3fr.
to - day.
C/G
A
Repeat and fade
One, two, three, four, five, six, sev - en, All good chil - dren go to heav - en.

Julia.

Words & Music by John Lennon & Paul McCartney

B
7fr.
Gm(add 9)
3fr.
Gm
3fr.
Last time to Coda
o - cean child, calls me.
wind - y smile, calls me.
si - lent cloud, touch me. (to Coda)
D
Bm7
F♯m
A
So I sing a song — of love, —
Ju - li-
Ju - - li-
D
C♯m
4fr.
a.
Her hair of
D
float - ing sky is shim - mer - ing,

Bm7
Bm6
F♯m7
glim - mer - ing,
in
the
F♯m6
F♯m(add D)
F♯m7
sun.
D
Bm7
Am
5fr.
Am7(add 9)
5fr.
Ju - li - a,
Ju - li - a,
B
7fr.
Gm(add 9)
3fr.
Gm
3fr.
morn - ing moon
touch
me.

D
Bm7
F♯m
So I sing a song— of love,— Ju -
A
D
D.S. al Coda
- li - a.
Coda
D
Bm7
F♯m
So I sing a song— of love,— Ju -
A
D
Bm7
- li - a,
T
A
B

Am
5fr.
Am(add 9)
5fr.
B
7fr.
(Hum) Mmm
Gm(add 9)
3fr.
Gm
3fr.
D
Bm7
calls
me.
So I sing a - song of love for
A
D
A
D
Ju - li - a,
Ju - li - a,
F♯m
A
Dmaj7
5fr.
Ju - - li - a.
rit.
rit.

You Won't See Me.

Words & Music by John Lennon & Paul McCartney

Moderately

D A

1. When I call

A B7

(Backing 2nd, 3rd times)

Oo *la* *la* *la*

Lay right hand palm across strings to stop the sound short on staccato.

you up, your line's engaged. I have had e-nough,
2. why you should want to hide. But I can't get through,

D A B7 D A

Oo *la* *la* *la* *Oo* *la* *la* *la* *Oo* *la* *la* *la*

so act your age. We have lost
my hands are tied. I won't want

A
5fr.
D
5fr.
Dm
5fr.
Oo
la la la
Oo
the time
that was so hard to find,
to stay,
I don't have much to say,
T
A
B
B T B T T T
A
B7
la la la
Oo
la la la
And I will lose my mind if
But I can turn a - way and
B T B T T T B
B
2 4 4 4 4 4 2 2
D
A
D
A
(Bkg.) You won't see me
you won't see me,
you won't see me,
cresc.
You won't see me.
You won't see me.
1.
2. A
You won't see me
You won't see me
2. I don't know
cresc.

D6
Dm6
Time af - ter time you re - fuse to e - ven lis -
T
A
B
B T B T
A
B7
ten. I would - n't mind if I knew
B T B T
B B T B B B T B
E7sus4
E7
(Backing): No I would - n't, no I would - n't
what I was miss - ing. Though the days
B B T B B B T B
A
B7
D
Oo la la la Oo
are few, they're filled with tears.
B
B
B

A
B7
la la la
Oo
la la la
And since I lost you it feels
D
A
A7
5fr.
Oo
la la la
Oo
like years.
Yes, it seems
so long
B T B T T T
Dm
5fr.
la la la
Oo
la la la
girl, since you've been gone,
And I just
B T B T T T
Oo
la la la
1. D
can't go on
if you won't see me,

D
A
(Bkg.) You won't see me
You won't see me
You won't see me.
cresc.
2.
D
A
You won't see me
You won't see me.
cresc.
D
A
A
You won't see me.
Oo
You won't see me.
(Backing only)
B7
D
A
B
Repeat and fade
la la la
Oo
la la la
B
B
B

We Can Work It Out.

Words & Music by John Lennon & Paul McCartney

Moderately slow

D Dsus4 D Dsus4

Try to see it my way, do I have to keep on talk - ing
Think of what you're say - ing, you can get it wrong and still you

CaddD D Dsus4 D

till I can't go on? While you see it your way,
think that it's all right. Think of what I'm say - ing,

Dsus4 CaddD D

run a risk of know - ing that our love may soon be gone.
we can work it out and get it straight, or say good - night.

G D G Asus4 A

We can work it out, we can work it out.

Bm
7fr.
Bm7
7fr.
Bm(addG)
7fr.
Life is ver - y short and there's no time
F♯sus4
6fr.
F♯
6fr.
Bm7
7fr.
Bm7
7fr.
for fuss - ing and fight - ing, my friend.
Bm(addG)
7fr.
Bm
7fr.
Bm
7fr.
Bm
7fr.
I have al - ways thought that it's a crime
Bm(addG)
7fr.
F♯sus4
6fr.
F♯
6fr.
Bm
7fr.
Bm7
7fr.
so I will ask you once a -
T
A
B

Bm(addG)
Bm
7fr.
D
Dsus4
D
gain.
Try to see it my way,
B
Dsus4
CaddD
D
Dsus4
D
on - ly time will tell if I am right or I am wrong.
While you see it your way
B
B
Dsus4
CaddD
D
there's a chance that we might fall a - part be - fore too long.
B
G
D
G
Asus4
A
D
G6/D
D
We can work it out,
we can work it out.
T
A
B

No Reply.

Words & Music by John Lennon & Paul McCartney

Em
Dm7
I know that you saw me, 'cause I looked up to
'Cause you walked hand in hand with an - oth - er
G7
C
3rd time to Coda
1.
see your face.
man in my place.
2. I tried to tel - e -
2.
C/G
E7
If I were you I'd re - al - ize that
give the lies that
A7
Dm
I love you more than
I heard be - fore when you

F
C/G
an - y oth - er guy.
gave me no re - ply.
T
A
B
B B B B B B
1.
2.
D.S. al Coda
And I'll for -
3. I tried to tel - e -
B B B B B B
C
Coda
Am
Em
No re - ply,
B
Fmaj7
C(add9)
No re - ply.

Getting Better.

Words & Music by John Lennon & Paul McCartney

G
C/G
G
C/G
Ah
Ah-oo
hold - ing me down, turn - ing me round,
gave me the word, I fin - al - ly heard, I'm
G
C/G
G
C
G
Fool - ish rules.
fill - ing me up with your rules.
do - ing the best that I can.
1.2. I've
C
F(add9)
Bet - ter.
got to ad - mit it's get - ting bet - ter; a lit - tle bet-
3. I ad - mit it's get - ting bet - ter; a lit - tle bet-
Em
F(add9)
It can't get no worse.
ter all the time.
ter all the time.
I

C
F(add9)
Bet - ter.
have to ad - mit it's get - ting bet - ter, it's get - ting bet -
Yes, I ad - mit it's get - ting bet - ter, it's get - ting bet -
Em
F(add9)
1. G
ter, since you've been mine.
ter, since you've been mine.
C
2.3. F C F C F C F C
(Group)
(2.) Me Get - ting so much bet - ter all the time.
C
F(add9)
It's get - ting bet - ter all the time.

Em
F(add9)
C
Bet - ter bet - ter, bet - ter.
It's get - ting bet - ter all the
T
A
B
F(add9)
Em
F(add9)
To Coda
time.
Bet - ter bet - ter, bet - ter.
G
G
I used to be cruel to my wom-
Tap right hand on front of guitar
for percussive sound
an, I beat her and kept her a - part from the things

G
that she loved.
Man, I was mean, but I'm chang-
ing my scene, and I'm do - ing the best that I can.
B B T B B T
D.S. al Coda
(take 3rd lyric and 3rd ending)
Coda
F C F C
Get - ting so much
bet - ter all the time.
Fade out
T
A
B

With A Little Help From My Friends.

Words & Music by John Lennon & Paul McCartney

Moderato
C
B7
E
E/B
B7
E
B/D♯
7fr.
F♯ m
What would you do___ if I sang___ out of tune___ would you stand___
What do I do___ when my love___ is a - way___ (Does it wor -
(Would you be - lieve___ in a love___ at first sight?)___ Yes, I'm cer -
B7
E
___ up and walk___ out on me?___
ry you to be___ a - lone?)___
tain that it hap - pens all the time.
(Lay side of right palm on strings to get a muffled sound)

B
F♯m
Lend me your ears and I'll sing you a song and I'll try
How do I feel by the end of the day (Are you sad
(What do you see when you turn out the light?) I can't tell
T
A
B
0
T
6
T
2
T
B
T
B7
E
not to sing out of key. Oh, I get by
be - cause you're on your own?) No, I get by
you, but I know it's mine. Oh, I get by
4
T
2
D
5fr.
A
5fr.
E
with a lit - tle help from my friends, Mm, I get high
with a lit - tle help from my friends, Mm, I get high
with a lit - tle help from my friends, Mm, I get high
D
5fr.
A
5fr.
E
3
with a lit - tle help from my friends Mm, I'm gon - na try
with a lit - tle help from my friends Mm, I'm gon - na try
with a lit - tle help from my friends Oh, I'm gon - na try

1.
A
E
B7
with a lit - tle help from my friends. (repeat to 2nd lyric)
with a lit - tle help from my friends. (to 2nd ending)
with a lit - tle help from my friends. (to 3rd ending)
T
A
B
2.3.
E
C♯m
4fr.
(Do you need an - y - bod -
(Do you need an - y - bod -
F♯7
E
D
A
C♯m
y?) I need some - bod - y to love (Could it be an - y - bod -
y?) I just need some - one to love (Could it be an - y - bod -
F♯7
E
D
A
To Coda
D.S. al Coda
y?) I want some - bod - y to love (repeat to sign)
y?) I want some - bod - y to love (to Coda)

Coda
A
D
5fr.
A
5fr.
Oh, I get by with a lit - tle help from my friends,
E
D
5fr.
A
5fr.
E
Mm, I'm gon - na try with a lit - tle help from my friends.
Oh, I get high
D
5fr.
A
5fr.
E
D
with a lit - tle help from my friends,
Yes, I get by with a lit - tle help from my friends,
A
C/G
Am6
E
with a lit - tle help from my friends.
T
A
B

You're Going To Lose That Girl.

Words & Music by John Lennon & Paul McCartney

E
G♯m7
4fr.
And I will take her out to - night, and I will
'Cause I will treat her right and then you'll be the
F♯m7
B7
E
I'm gon - na treat her kind.
You're not the on - ly one.
treat her kind.
lone - ly one.
You're gon - na
C♯m7
4fr.
Yes, yes, you're gon - na lose that girl.
lose that girl,
You're gon - na
B
F♯m7
1. B7
Yes, yes, you're gon - na lose that girl.
lose that girl.
B

2. B7
F♯m7
(Bkg) lose that girl.
Yes, yes you're gon - na
girl, you're gon - na lose.
D
G
lose that girl.
(Group) I'll make a point of
B
C
G
Watch what you do.
tak - ing her a - way from you.
Yeah,
C
F
To Coda
the way you treat her, what else can I do?

E
G♯m7
4fr.
F♯m7
(Solo)
You're gon - na
1. B7
2. B7
E
Yes, yes, you're gon - na
lose that girl.
lose that girl. You're gon - na lose that girl.
(Solo Voice)
C♯m7
4fr.
F♯m7
B7
D.S. al Coda
lose that girl.
Yes, yes, you're gon - na
lose that girl.
You're gon - na lose that girl. You're gon - na
Coda
E
G♯m7
4fr
F♯m7
She's gon - na
If you don't take her out to - night she's gon - na change her mind.

B7
E
G♯m7
4fr.
change her mind.
And I will take her out to - night, and I will
F♯m7
B7
E
I'm gon - na treat her kind.
Yes, yes, you're gon - na
treat her kind.
You're gon - na lose that girl,
C♯m7
4fr.
F♯m7
B7
lose that girl.
Yes, yes, you're gon - na lose that girl.
You're gon - na lose that girl.
You're gon - na
F♯m7
D
E
Yes, yes, you're gon - na lose that girl.
lose that girl.
T
A
B

It Won't Be Long.

Words & Music by John Lennon & Paul McCartney

C
E
Here am I sit - ting all on my own.
Ev - 'ry day I've done noth - ing but cry.
Now I know that you won't leave me no more.
T
A
B
C♯m
4fr.
(Yeah) (Yeah) (Yeah)
It won't be long yeah, yeah, yeah, It won't be
E
C♯m
4fr.
To Coda
(Yeah) (Yeah) (Yeah) (Yeah)
long yeah, yeah, yeah. It won't be long yeah, till
A
A♯dim
E
I be - long to you. Since you

E
D♯+
Bm6/D
left me I'm so a - lone. Now you're com - ing, you're
C♯7
Am/C
B7
com - ing on home. I'll be good like I know I should, You're com - ing
F♯m7
1.
B7
2.
B7
D.S. al Coda
home, you're com - ing home. home. So
Coda
A
rit.
Slowly
G
F♯
F
Emaj7
I be - long to you.
T
A
B

Hey Jude.

Words & Music by John Lennon & Paul McCartney

D
F
G
B♭
D
F
get her.__ The min-ute you let her un-der your skin, then you be-gin_
get her.__ Re-mem-ber to let her in-to your heart, then you can start_
T
A
B
B B T B B T
A7
C7
D
F
D7
F7
__ to make it___ bet-ter.__ And an-y time_ you feel the pain_
__ to make it___ bet-ter.__ So let it out_ and let it in_
B B T B B T B B T
3
G
B♭
Em7
Gm7
A7
C7
__ Hey Jude,_ re-frain,__ don't car-ry the world_ up-on__ your shoul-
__ Hey Jude,_ be-gin,__ you're wait-ing for some-one to__ per-form_
B B B B
D
F
D7
F7
G
B♭
ders.___ For well you know that it's a fool who plays_ it cool_
__ with.___ And don't you know that it's just you Hey Jude,_ you'll do._
B B B B B B B B B B

Em7 A7 D
Gm7 C7 F
By mak - ing his world a lit - tle cold - er. Da da da
The move - ment you need is on your shoul - der. Da da da
D7 A7
F7 C7
1. 2.
D.S. al Coda
da da da da da da.
da da da da da da.
Hey
Hey
Coda
A7 D
C7 F
to make it bet - ter, bet - ter, bet - ter, bet - ter, bet - ter, bet - ter, Oh
D C/G G D
F E♭ B♭ F
Repeat and fade
Da da da da da da da da da da da Hey Jude.

I'm So Tired.

Words & Music by John Lennon & Paul McCartney

F♯m7
Dm7
Dm6
Dm7
A
5fr.
but double tempo feel
know what you would do.
You'd say I'm put - ting you on, but it's
E7
no joke, it's do - ing me harm. You know I can't sleep, I can't stop my brain, you know it's
D
To Coda
three weeks, I'm go - ing in - sane. You know I'd give you ev - 'ry - thing I've got for a lit - tle peace of mind.
A
Tempo I
A
G♯
I'm so tired, I'm
T
A
B

D
E
A
F♯m7
feel - ing so up - set.
Al - though I'm so tired,
D
E7
A
E+
I'll have an - oth - er cig - a - rette, And curse Sir Wal - ter Ra - leigh, he was
D.S. al Coda
F♯m
Dm7
Dm6
Dm7
5fr.
such a stu - pid get!
Coda
A
I'd
D
A
give you ev - 'ry - thing I've got for a lit - tle peace of mind.

Tell Me Why.

Words & Music by John Lennon & Paul McCartney

Em7
A7
D
1. Well, I gave you ev - 'ry - thing I had,
2. If it's some - thing that I've said or done,
Bm7
Em7
A7
(harmony)
But you left me sit - ing on my own.
Tell me what, and I'll a - pol - o - gize.
D
Did you have to treat me oh so bad?
If you don't I real - ly can't go on
Bm7
Em7
A7
(harmony)
All I do is hang my head and moan. Tell me (repeat)
Hold - ing back these tears in my eyes. Tell me (cont.)
T
A
B

D
Bm7
Em7
A7
why you cried, and why you lied to
B
D
Em7
A7
D
Bm7
me. Tell me why you cried,
B
B
Em7
To Coda
A7
D6
D7
and why you lied to me. Well, I
B
G7
A7
beg you on my bend-ed knees, If you'll on-ly lis-ten to my pleas.

D
Is there an-y-thing I can do 'Cause I
G7
A7
D
real-ly can't stand it, I'm so in love with you.
A7
D.S. al Coda
Tell me
Lay left hand lightly across strings for × sound.
Coda
A7
lied to
D6
B♭7
A13
A7+5
D
me.
TAB

Why Don't We Do It In The Road.

Words & Music by John Lennon & Paul McCartney

D
10fr.
A
5fr.
No one will be watch-ing us; Why
G
3fr.
D7
don't we do it in the road?
Why don't we do it in the road?
(Place left hand lightly across strings for percussive sound)
D7
Why don't we do it in the road?
Why don't we do it in the road?

G
3fr.
Why don't we do it in the road?
D
10fr.
A
5fr.
No one will be watch-ing us; Why
G
3fr.
D7
don't we do it in the road?
Oh,
why don't we do it in the road?
T
A
B

Why don't we do it in the road?
G
3fr.
Why don't we do it, do it in the road?
D7
Why don't we do it in the road?
No
A
5fr.
G
3fr.
N.C.
D7
one will be watch-ing us;
Why don't we do it in the road?
T
A
B

I'm Happy Just To Dance With You.

Words & Music by John Lennon & Paul McCartney

C
Am7
Dm7
G7
E
C♯m7
F♯m7
B7
fun - ny try and un - der - stand.
wan - na dance with you all night.
There is
In this
T
A
B
F
C
Am7
A
E
C♯m7
real - ly noth - ing else I'd rath - er do,
world there's noth - ing I would rath - er do,
'Cause I'm
Dm
G+
1.C
G
2.C
F♯m
B+
E
B
E
hap - py just to dance with you.
2. I don't you.
Just to
Am7
Dm
E
Am
C♯m7
F♯m
G♯
C♯m
dance with you.
(Oh oh)
(Backing, 2nd time)
is ev - 'ry - thing I
T B T

Dm E Am
F♯m G C♯m
(Bkg.) (Oh oh)
need. Be - fore this dance is through, I think I'll
Dm E Dm G7
F♯m G♯ F♯m B7
love you too, I'm so hap - py when you dance with
C G7 C Am7
E B7 E C♯m7
me. If some - bod - y tries to take my place,
Dm7 G7 C Am7
F♯m7 B7 E C♯m7
let's pre - tend we just can't see his face

Dm7
G7
F
C
Am7
F♯m7
B7
A
E
C♯m7
In this world there's noth-ing I would rath-er do
'Cause I'm hap-py just to dance with you.
I've dis-cov-ered I'm in love with
Just to
you.
T
A
B
Dm
G+
C
Am
F♯m
B+
E
C♯m
1.
2.
Dm
E
Dm
G+
Am
F♯m
G
F♯m
B+
C♯m
(Bkg.)(Oh oh)
'Cause I'm hap-py just to dance with you,
Dm7
E
Dm
G7
C6
F♯m7
G♯
F♯m
B7
E6
(Bkg. & Solo)
Oh, oh, oh, oh, oh!

Baby You're A Rich Man.

Words & Music by John Lennon & Paul McCartney

Moderately
G7
3fr.
C/G
3fr.
Play 4 times
Rest right hand on strings as you play for a muffled effect for the entire song.
Lift pressure of left hand for percussive sound
mf
G
3fr.
C/G
3fr.
G7
3fr.
1. How does it feel— to be one of the beau - ti - ful peo - ple?
2. How does it feel— to be one of the beau - ti - ful peo - ple?
3. How does it feel— to be one of the beau - ti - ful peo - ple?
F
G7
3fr.
Now that you know— who you are—— what do you want— to be?——
How of - ten have— you been there,—— of - ten e - nough— to know.——
Tuned to a nat - u - ral E,—— hap - py to be—— that way.——
C/G
3fr.
G7
3fr.
Lift muffled sound for this one measure
And have you trav - eled ver - y far,——
What did you see—— when you were there——
Now that you've found—— an - oth - er key——

F
G7
3fr.
C/G
3fr.
far as the eye can see? (repeat to verse 2)
noth-ing that does-n't show? (continue to chorus)
what are you going to play? (continue to chorus)
Lift muffled sound for this one measure
T
A
B
G
C
Ba-by you're a rich man, Ba-by you're a rich man,
No muffled sound for this section
G
C
B♭dim
G7/B
Ba-by you're a rich man, too. You keep all your mon-ey in a
C
G
3fr.
C
big brown bag in-side a zoo; What a thing to do!

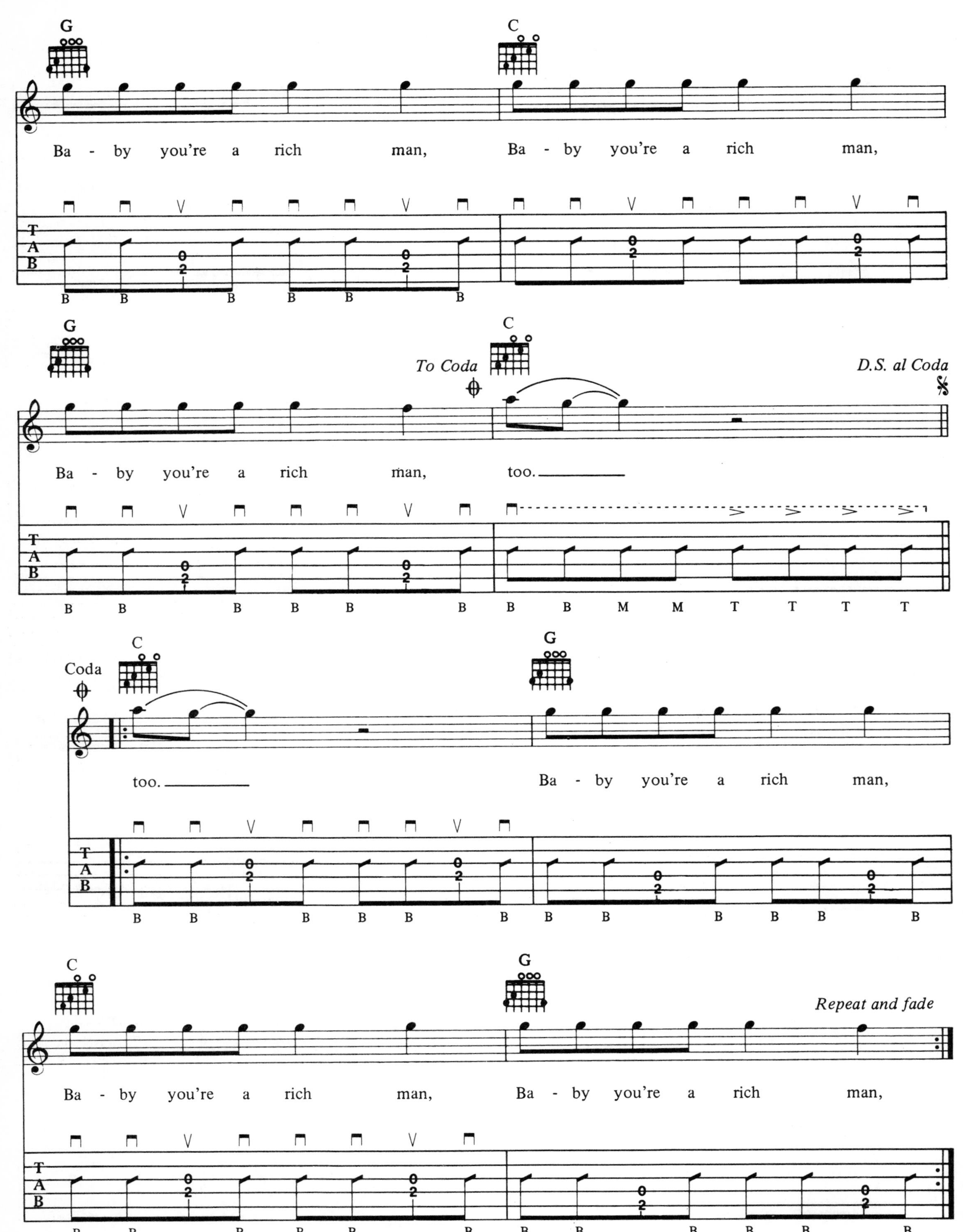
G
C
Ba - by you're a rich man, Ba - by you're a rich man,
T
A
B
0
2
B B B B B B
To Coda
D.S. al Coda
Ba - by you're a rich man, too.
B B B B B B B B M M T T T T
Coda
too.
Ba - by you're a rich man,
Repeat and fade
Ba - by you're a rich man, Ba - by you're a rich man,

Help!

Words & Music by John Lennon & Paul McCartney

F♯m
2fr.
D
G
A
Back to regular strum
I never needed anybody's help in any way.
My independence seems to vanish in the haze.
C♯m
4fr.
But now these days are gone, I'm not so self-assured,
But ev'ry now and then I feel so insecure,
F♯m
2fr.
D
G
A
Now I find I've changed my mind, I've opened up the doors.
I know that I just need you like I've never done before.
Bm
Bm/A
Help me if you can, I'm feeling down,
And I do
T
A
B

G
G/F♯
— ap - pre - ci - ate you be-ing 'round.
B
E7
Help me get my feet back on the ground. Won't you
B
A
Tacet
please please help me?
1.2.
A
B
3.
F♯m
2fr.
A6
— Help me, Help me, Help me! Oo.
B

A Hard Day's Night.

Words & Music by John Lennon & Paul McCartney

1.
G
C9
To Coda
G
feel al - right. 2. You know I
be O. K.
2. G
Bm
Em
When I'm home
ev - 'ry - thing seems to be al -
Bm
G
right,
When I'm home
Em
C
D
D.S. al Coda
feel - ing you hold - ing me tight,
tight, yeah, 3. It's been a
T
A
B

Coda
G
F
1.
G
(scream)
2.
G
C
D
So why I love to come home 'Cause when I get you a - lone you know I'll
G
C9
G
Bm
be O. K. When I'm home
Em
Bm
ev - 'ry - thing seems to be al - right,

G
When I'm home
Em
C
D
D.S. al Coda
feel - ing you hold - ing me tight, tight, yeah. 3. It's been a
Coda
G
C9
You know I feel al right,
G
CaddD
N.C.
You know I feel al - right.
Repeat and fade

I Should Have Known Better.

Words & Music by John Lennon & Paul McCartney

2.3.
C
B
Em
C
Can't you see?
That when I tell you that I love
Em
B
Em
C
you,
Oh!
You're gon - na say you love me too,
G
G7
C
D
hoo hoo hoo hoo, oh.
And when I ask you to be mi-
[mine]
G
Em
C
D
Last time to Coda
ah - ha - hine
you're gon - na say you love me, too.
T
A
B
B B B B
B

G D G D G D
3. So wo I
G D G D G D
should have re - al - ized a lot of things be - fore.
If this is
G D Em C
love, you got - ta give me more; give me more,
hey, hey, hey,
D G D G D
give me more.
TAB
B B B B

G
D
G
D
G
D
3fr.
(Solo)
G6
D
G
D
Em
C
D
G6
G
D
G
D
D.S. al Coda
So— wo—
Coda
G
D
G
D
G
Repeat and fade
D
G
You love me, too.—

Eight Days A Week.

Words & Music by John Lennon & Paul McCartney

Brightly in 4

Bm
E
D
Hold me, love me. I ain't got noth-in' but
B
E
G
D
love, babe, eight days a week.
B
A
Bm
Eight days a week, I love
T B T B T B T B
E
you. Eight days a week is
T T T T

G6
A
D
not e - nough to show I care.
Ooh I need your
Love you ev - 'ry
3
3
B
E
G
D
love, babe, guess you know it's true.
day, girl, al - ways on my mind.
B
E
G
Hope you need my love, babe, just like I need you.
One thing I can say, girl, love you all the time.
B
D
Bm
G6
Hold me, love me.
B

Bm
E
D
Hold me, love me. I ain't got noth - in' but
T
A
B
B
E
G
D
love, babe, eight days a week.
B
G
D
G
D
Eight days a week. Eight days a week.
B
D
5fr.
E/D
7fr.
G/D
10fr.
D
5fr.

Run For Your Life.

Words & Music by John Lennon & Paul McCartney

Bm
lit - tle girl, or I(you) won't know where I am.
life try - in' just to make you toe the line.
mined and I'd rath - er see you dead.
T
A
B
D
(main voice: heavier notes)
E
You'd bet - ter run for your life if you can, lit - tle girl;
B
D
E
Hide your head in the sand lit - tle girl,
Bm
Em
F♯7
Bm
4th time to Coda
Catch you with an - oth - er man, that's the end - a, lit - tle

1.3.
D7
girl.
2.
2. Well, you girl
4. I'd
Use 3rd finger on slide.
D7
(Solo)
G

D7
A7
D
D.S. al Coda
(use 3rd and 4th lyrics)
Coda
Bm
D7
girl.
Repeat and fade
No, no, no.

Little Child.

Words & Music by John Lennon & Paul McCartney

2.
F♯7
B7
E
ba - by take a chance with me.
1. If you
T
A
B
B
E
B
want some - one to make you feel so fine, then we'll
by my side you're the on - ly one, don't you
B B B B B B
E
E7
have some fun when you're mine all mine. So come
run and hide, just come on, come on. Yeah, come
B B B B B B
F♯
B
3
on, come on, come on,
on, come on, come on,
Lit - tle child,
B B B B B B

E
A
lit - tle child,
lit - tle child,
won't you dance with me?
E7
B7
A
I'm so sad and lone - ly,
F♯ 7
B7
To Coda
E7
ba - by take a chance with me.
(Solo)
Wow! (shout)
E7
Emphasize top note of each strum
to bring out melody.

A(add9)
E7
B7
A
F♯7
B7
D.S. al Coda
2. When you're
Coda
E
C♯7
4fr.
F♯7
B7
E
C♯7
4fr.
Repeat and fade
Oh, yeah, ba - by take a chance with me. Oh, yeah,

All My Loving.

Words & Music by John Lennon & Paul McCartney

1.
2.3.
A
B7
E
C♯m
C+
5fr.
7fr.
4fr.
send all my lov - ing to you. I'll pre -
you. All my lov - ing I will send to
you, All my lov - ing, dar - ling, I'll be true.
Last time to Coda
T
A
B

A
Emphasize top note at all times
to bring out melody line.
Keep chord positions down and play off of them.
5fr.
E
4fr.
F♯m
B
7fr.
E
4fr.
D.S. al Coda
3. Close your
Coda
E
4fr.
C♯m
4fr.
(true.) All my lov - ing,
E
All my lov - ing. All my
C♯m
4fr.
E
lov - ing, I will send to you.

Carry That Weight.

Words & Music by John Lennon & Paul McCartney

F
Dm
E7
Am
Pick up string while bending upward.
shake
Dm7
Dm
G
I never give you my pillow,
I only send you my
C
Fmaj7
invitations.
And in the middle of the
Dm
E7
Am
G
C/G
G
celebrations, I break down.

C/G
G7
Boy, you're gon - na car - ry that weight, car - ry that weight a long
C/G
G7
time.
Boy, you're gon - na car - ry that weight,
C
G
car - ry that weight, a long time.
A
C
G
A

I'm A Loser.

Words & Music by John Lennon & Paul McCartney

F
G
nev - er have crossed.
wear - ing a frown.
left it too late.
She was a girl
My tears are fall
And so it's true
Dm
5fr.
F
G
in a mil - lion, my friend.
ing like rain from the sky
pride comes be - fore a fall
Dm
5fr.
F
I should have known she would win in the end.
Is it for her or my - self that I cry?
I'm tell - ing you so that you won't lose all.
G
Am7
D7
I'm a los - er, and I lost
T
A
B

Am7
D7
G
— some - one who's near — to me. I'm a los —
Em
Am7
F
D7
er, and I'm not what I ap - pear — to be. —
G
Bring out top note on all accented chords
Dm
Fmaj7
1. G
2.G
Am
5fr.
D6
7fr.
Am
5fr.
D6
7fr.
(Fade out on last time)
Em7♭5
5fr.
Em
C
8fr.
D
5fr.

Good Day Sunshine.

Words & Music by John Lennon & Paul McCartney

Moderate barrel house tempo
E
f
B
F♯
7fr.
Good day sun - shine, Good day sun - shine, Good day sun - shine
E7
I need to laugh and when the sun is out I've got some-thing I can
And then we'd lie be-neath a shad-y tree, I love her and she's
mf
A
F♯ 7
B7
T
A
B

A
F♯7
B7
laugh a-bout. I feel good in a spe-cial way,
lov-ing me. She feels good - she knows she's look-ing fine,
T
A
B
B
0 4 3 2 2
E7
A
B
7fr.
F♯
I'm in love and it's a sun-ny day.
I'm so proud to know that she is mine.
Good day sun-
B B B
B
7fr.
F♯
Last time to Coda
shine, Good day sun - shine,
B 2 4 2
B B B
B 2 4 2
E7
A
F♯7
Good day sun - shine. We take a walk the sun is
B B B
B
B
0 4 3 2 2

* Rock fingers back and forth from left to right for tremolo.

Can't Buy Me Love.

Words & Music by John Lennon & Paul McCartney

C
G
makes you feel al - right.
got I'll give to you.
'Cause I don't care too
'Cause I don't care too
F7
C
much for mon - ey, for mon - ey can't buy me love.
much for mon - ey, for mon - ey can't buy me love.
I'll
C
Em
Am
Can't buy me love,
ev -
C
Em
'ry - bod - y tells me so.
Can't buy me love,
T
A
B

Am
Dm7
G
no no no
no!
C
Say you don't need no dia - mond rings and I'll be sat - is - fied,
B
F7
C
Tell me that you want the kind of things that mon - ey just can't buy.
G
F7
To Coda
I don't care too much for mon - ey,
T
A
B

F7
C
mon - ey can't buy me love.
B
B
C7
B (Scream)
T
F7
C7
G
3fr.
F
D.S. al Coda

Coda
F7
C
mon - ey can't buy me love.
Can't buy me love
Em
Am
Em
love
Am
Dm7
can't buy me love.
G
C
C
T
A
B

She Came In Through The Bathroom Window.

Words & Music by John Lennon & Paul McCartney

D
10fr.
A
banks of her own la - goon.
steal but she could not rob.
Did - n't an - y - bod - y tell
Dm
A
5fr.
her?
Did - n't an - y - bod - y see?
Dm
G7
3fr.
C
8fr.
To Coda
Sun - day's on the phone to Mon - day,
G7
3fr.
C
A
5fr.
Tues - day's on the phone to me.
She said she'd al - ways been a

D
10fr.
A
5fr.
danc - er,
she worked in fif - teen clubs a
D
10fr.
A
5fr.
day.
And though she thought I knew the
D
10fr.
D
10fr.
D.S. al Coda
an - swer,
Well, I knew but I could not say.
Coda
G7
3fr.
C
A
9fr.
Tues - day's on the phone to me,
oh yeah!
B B B B

Back In The USSR.

Words & Music by John Lennon & Paul McCartney

Moderate Boogie - Rock tempo

E7
f
E7
E7/4
A
5fr.
D
5fr.
Flew in from Mi - a - mi Beach, B. O. A. C., Did -
Been a - way so long I hard - ly knew the place, Gee
C
3fr.
D
5fr.
n't get to bed last night. On
it's good to get back home. Leave

A
5fr.
D
5fr.
the way the pa - per bag was on my knee, Man
it till to - mor - row to un - pack my case, Hon -
C
3fr.
D
5fr.
I had a dread - ful flight.
ey, dis - con - nect the phone.
I'm back in the U. S. S. R.,
A
5fr.
C
8fr.
D
10fr.
You don't know how luck - y you are, boy.
1.
D
10fr.
A
D
2fr.
E♭
3fr.
E
4fr.
Back in the U. S. S. R.
Release left hand pressure on A chord for 1st sound.
Lay left hand lightly across strings for 2nd sound.

2.
G/E
Back in the U. S., Back in the U. S., Back in the U. S. S. R.
T T T T T T T T T T
A
5fr.
D
Well, the U - kraine girls real - ly
B B B B B B B
knock me out. They leave the West be - hind. And
A
D
F♯m/C♯
Am/C
B7
E7
Mos - cow girls make me sing and shout that Geor - gia's al - ways on my - mi - mi -
B

D7
A
B7
E7
mi - mi - mi - mi - mi - mi - mind.
T
A
B
A(addD)
9fr.
D
10fr.
C
8fr.
1.
2.
5fr.
I'm back in the U. S. S. R.,
You don't know how luck - y you are,
boy.
Back in the U. S. S. R.

A
5fr.
D
Well, the U - kraine girls real - ly
B B B B B B B
A
knock me out. They leave the West be - hind. And
D
F♯m/C♯
Am/C
B7
E7
Mos - cow girls make me sing and shout that Geor - gia's al - ways on my - mi - mi -
B
D7
A
B7
E7
mi - mi - mi - mi - mi - mi - mind.
B B B B B B B

A
5fr.
D
5fr.
Show me 'round your snow - peaked moun - tains way down south, Take
Am7
5fr.
D
5fr.
me to your dad - dy's farm. Let
A
5fr.
D
5fr.
me hear your bal - a - lai - kas ring - ing out, Come
Am7
5fr.
D
5fr.
and keep your com - rade warm. I'm back in the U. S. S. R.
3
T
A
B

A
5fr.
C
3fr.
D
10fr.
You don't know how luck - y you are,
boy.
A
Back in the U. S. S. R.
D
E♭
E
2fr.
3fr.
4fr.
A
Yeah!

Any Time At All.

Words & Music by John Lennon & Paul McCartney

D
A/C♯
5fr.
1. If you need some - bod - y to love
2. If the sun has fad - ed a - way
T
A
B
B
B
B
B
Bm
Gm/B♭
just look in - to my eyes;
I'll try to make it shine;
B
B
B
D/A
A7/C♯
5fr.
I'll be there to make you feel
There is noth - in' I won't
B
B
D
A/C♯
5fr.
right. If you're feel - ing sor - ry and sad,
do. When you need a shoul - der to cry on,

Bm
Gm/B♭
D/A
I'd real - ly sym - pa - thize.
I hope it will be mine.
Don't you be sad, just
Call me to - night and
B
B
B
A7/C♯
5fr.
D
call me to - night.
I'll come to you.
1.
2.
D.S. al Coda
An - y time at
An - y time at
Coda
Em7
F♯m(add 9)
G6(add9)
Em
F♯m(add 9)
Solo (Emphasize top notes on all accented strums)

G6(add9)
A
Ab
G
3fr.
Ab
4fr.
A
5fr.
Ab
G
3fr.
A
5fr.
G
3fr.
A
5fr.
D
An - y time at
Bm
all,
D
An - y time at all,
A
B
B
B
B

Bm
An - y time at all, all you got - ta do is
G
A7
D
call and I'll be there.
G
An - y time at all, all you got - ta do is
M
A7
D
call and I'll be there.

I'm Looking Through You.

Words & Music by John Lennon & Paul McCartney

Em D C G C D
Fm Eb Db Ab Db Eb
You don't_ look dif - f'rent, but you have changed,
You don't_ sound dif - f'rent, I've learned the game,
G C Am7 C7
Ab Db Bbm7 Db7
I'm look-ing through_ you, you're not_ the same.
G C G C G C
Ab Db Ab Db Ab Db
3fr.
G C C G
Ab Db Db Ab
Why, tell me why_ did you_ not treat me right?_

C
Db
Dsus4
Ebsus
Love has a nas - ty hab - it of dis - ap - pear - ing
D G C Am7 Em
Eb Ab Db Bbm7 Fm
o - ver night.
3. You're think - ing of me the same old
4. I'm look-ing through you, where did you go?
B
D G C Am7 Em
Eb Ab Db Bbm7 Fm
way; You were a - bove me, but not to - day.
I thought I knew you, what did I
D Em D C G C
Eb Fm Eb Db Ab Db
know? The on - ly dif - f'rence is you're down
You don't look dif - f'rent but you have

D
G
C
Am7
E♭
A♭
D♭
B♭m7
there; I'm look-ing through you
changed; I'm look-ing through you
C7
1. G
C
D♭7
and you're no-where.
you're not the same.
2. G
Voice ad lib: Yeah! Well, ba-by you've changed.
Repeat and fade
Ah, I'm look-ing through you . . .

Hello Goodbye.

Words & Music by John Lennon & Paul McCartney

A♭
4fr.
C
why you say good - bye, I say hel - lo, hel - lo, hel - lo.
F
B♭
C
I don't know why you say good - bye, I say hel - lo.
F
C
G7
I say high You say low You say why and
You say yes I say no You say stop and
cresc.
Am
G7
Am
5fr.
I say I don't know
I say go go go
Oh Oh no

G7
7fr.
G
3fr.
F
5fr.
You say good - bye and I say hel - lo
C
F
A♭
4fr.
hel - lo hel - lo I don't know why you say good - bye I say hel - lo
C
F
B♭
To Coda
C
hel - lo hel - lo I don't know why you say good-bye I say hel - lo
F
C
Solo
Why why why

G7
Am
G
D.S. al Coda
why why why do you say good - bye good - bye
C
C/B
C/A
C/G
F
5fr.
Coda
Hel - lo hel - lo I don't know
A♭
4fr.
A♭
A♭/G
why you say good - bye I say hel - lo
A♭/F♯
A♭/F
C
C/G
Repeat and fade
Hel - lo Hel - lo he - ba hel - lo - a

She's A Woman.

Words & Music by John Lennon & Paul McCartney

Fairly bright, with a strong back beat
E7
D7
f
T
A
B
A7
A7
D7
A7
Release left hand pressure of sound.
1.3.4. My love don't give me pres - ents,
2. She don't give boys the eye.
A7
D7
A7
I know that she's no peas - ant.
She hates to see me cry.

D7
On - ly ev - er has to give me love for - ev - er and for - ev - er;
She is hap - py just to hear me say that I will nev - er leave her;
A7
D7
A7
My love don't give me pres - ents.
She don't give boys the eye.
E7
D7
Turn me on when I get lone - ly Peo - ple tell me that she's on - ly
She will nev - er make me jeal ous, Give me all her time as well as
A7
D7
4th time to Coda
A7
1.
E7
fool - in', I know she is - n't.
lov - in', Don't ask me why.
T
A
B

2.
A7
C♯m
4fr.
F♯7
2fr.
She's a wom - an who un - der - stands;
C♯m
4fr.
D
E
3 E7
She's a wom - an who loves her man.
A7
5fr.
(Solo)
D
10fr.
C
8fr.
D
A
5fr.
G
3fr.
D
A

E
4fr.
D
7fr.
D7
7fr.
A7
C♯m
4fr.
F♯7
2fr.
C♯m
4fr.
She's a wom - an who un - der - stands;
She's a wom - an who
D
E
D.S. al Coda
loves her man.
A7
Coda
Repeat and fade
She's a wom - an,
She's a wom -

Hold Me Tight.

Words & Music by John Lennon & Paul McCartney

1.
2.
F/C
C
A♭
F
4fr.
you.
Don't know
A♭
F
Dm
Gm
4fr.
5fr.
3fr.
what it means to hold you tight.
Be - ing here a - lone to - night with you,
G
C7
F
B♭
It feels so right.
Now, hold me tight,
So hold me tight,
G7
C7
F
B♭
3fr.
tell me I'm the on - ly one, and then I might
let me go on lov - ing you, to - night, to - night,
T
A
B

G7
3fr.
C7
F
F7
nev - er be the lone - ly one.
mak - ing love to on - ly you.
So hold (hold) me tight, (me tight) to - night,
Bb
Bbm
F
(to - night) to - night, (to - night) it's you,
Bbm
F
1.
Ab
4fr.
you, you, you,
Don't
2.
Ab
4fr.
Gb
F
Ab
4fr.
Gb
F
hoo hoo, you, hoo hoo.
T
A
B

I Will.

Words & Music by John Lennon & Paul McCartney

Bb C6 Dm Gm C7
3fr.
Love you for - ev - er and for - ev - er, Love you with all my heart.
F F7 Bb C6 Dm
Love you when - ev - er we're to - geth - er,
G C F Dm7
8fr.
Love you when we're a - part. And when at last I find
Gm7 C7 F Dm7 Am F7 Bb C7
3fr.
you, your song will fill the air; Sing it loud so I can hear.

Dm Bb F Bb C7 Dm Bb F Bb C7
— you, — Make it eas - y to — be near — you, For the things — you do — en - dear —
M M M
2
Dm Bb F Bb C7 Db
— you to — me, Ah — you know — I will. —
F F7
I will. —
Bb C6 Dm Gm C7 F
3fr.
La la la la — la la — la la — la la la la la la la la. —
B B B B B B B B B B

It's Only Love.

Words & Music by John Lennon & Paul McCartney

Moderato
C Am C Am
C Em/B B♭ F Gsus G+
1. I get high when I see you go by, My oh my.
2. Is it right that you and I should fight ev - 'ry night?
C Em/B B♭ F Gsus Gsus
When you sigh, my, my in - side just flies, but - ter - flies.
Just the sight of you makes night - time bright, ver - y bright.
F G C Am
Why am I so shy when I'm be - side you?
Hav - en't I the right to make it up girl?
It's on - ly

B♭
G7
C
Am
love and that is all,
Why should I feel the way I do?
It's on - ly
T
A
B
B♭
G7
F
1.
G7
love, and that is all,
but it's so hard lov - ing you.
2.
G7
F
G7
C
Am
you, Yes, it's so hard lov - ing you lov - ing you.
C
Am
C
Am
C

Girl.

Words & Music by John Lennon & Paul McCartney

C
Em
Dm
G7
C
Em
E♭
Gm
Fm
B♭7
E♭
Gm
Girl,
Girl,
Girl,
Hold the pick loosely & low so only a little is showing.
Let your fingers & pick strum the strings for a "brushing" effect.
1. Dm
G7
2. Dm
G7
Fm
B♭7
Fm
B♭7
When I
Dm
A
Fm
C
Release pressure of left hand for staccato.
Allow open strings to ring through.
She's the kind of girl who puts you down when friends are there, you feel a
Dm
A
Dm
Fm
C
Fm
fool.
When you say she's look - ing good, she

A
Dm
F
C
Fm
Ab
acts as if it's un - der - stood, she's cool,
ooh,
ooh,
ooh,
C
Em
Dm
G7
C
Em
Eb
Gm
Fm
Bb7
Eb
Gm
Girl,
Girl,
Girl,
"Brushed" effect
Dm
Am
E7
Am
To Coda
Fm
Cm
G7
Cm
1. Was she told when she was young that pain would lead to plea - sure?
(no lyric on D.S.)
Dm
C
E7
Am
E7
Fm
Eb
G7
Cm
G7
Did she un - der - stand it when they said
That a man must break his back to earn his

Am
Cm
Dm
Fm
Am
Cm
D.S. al Coda
day of lei - sure? Will she still be - lieve it when he's dead? Ah,
Coda
E7
G7
Release left hand pressure for staccato.
For open string staccatos, use finger that
your releasing pressure on to touch open string.
1.
C
E♭
2.
Em
Gm
G7
B♭7
Repeat and fade
Girl,
Girl.
"Brushed" effect.
B B B B B

Your Mother Should Know.

Words & Music by John Lennon & Paul McCartney

Am
F
Let's all get up and dance to a song that was a
T
A
B
B
A7/E
Dm
G7
hit be - fore your moth - er was born.
Though she was born a long,
C
C/B
A7
D7
long time a - go, your moth - er should know,
G7
C
your moth - er should know.

E
Am
F
Dm
G(add9)
C
E7
1.
2. Sing it a - gain:
Am
F
A7/E
Lift up your hearts and sing me a song that was a hit be - fore your
Da da da da da da da da da da da da da da da da
Dm
G7
C
C/B
moth - er was born.
da da da da.
Though she was born a long, long time a - go,

A7
D7
G7
your moth - er should know,
your moth - er should know.
B
C
A7
D7
Your moth - er should know,
B
G7
1.C
E
2.C
your moth - er should know.
B
B
B
A7
D7
G7
C
Your moth - er should know,
your moth - er should know.
B

Fixing A Hole.

Words & Music by John Lennon & Paul McCartney

2.
Fm7
B♭
F
C11
And it real - ly does - n't mat - ter if I'm wrong,
I'm right where I be - long, I'm right where I be - long.
C
G7
See the peo - ple stand - ing there who dis - a - gree and nev - er win and
Sil - ly peo - ple run a - round, who wor - ry me and nev - er ask me
won - der why they don't get in my door.
why they don't get past my door.
(Hold 2nd & 3rd fingers down on chord, & use 1st finger for guitar line.)
I'm
I'm
T
A
B

F
C+
Fm
C+
paint - ing a room in a col - or - ful way, and
tak - ing the time for a num - ber of things that
Fm7
Fm6
To Coda
when my mind is wan - der - ing there I will
weren't im - por - tant yes - ter - day. And I still
(to Coda)
Fm
Fm7
B♭9
Fm7
go.
Oo oo oo ah
Fm6
F
C+
Fm
C+
Fm7
ah hey hey hey
(Solo)

Fm6
Fm7
Fm6
Fm7
Fm6
D.S. al Coda
And it
Coda
Fm
Fm6
go.
Fm7
Fm6
Oo oo oo oo oo.
I'm

Fm7
Fm6
fix - ing a hole where the rain gets in, and
Fm7
B♭9
stops my mind from wan - der - ing where it will
Fm7
Fm6
go,
where it will
Fm7
Fm6
Repeat and fade
go.
I'm

Eleanor Rigby.

Words & Music by John Lennon & Paul McCartney

Moderately, with a steady beat
C
Ah look at all the lone - ly peo -
Em
ple!
C
Ah look at all
the lone - ly peo - ple!
Em
Em
El - ea - nor Rig - by, picks up the rice in the church where a wed - ding has been,

C
Em
Em
7fr.
lives in a dream.
Waits at the win - dow,
T
A
B
wear-ing the face that she keeps in a jar by the door,
C
8fr.
Em
7fr.
Em7
Em6
Em(♭6)
who is it for?
All the lone - ly peo - ple, where do they all come from?
Em
Em7
Em6
Em(♭6)
Em
All the lone - ly peo - ple, where do they all be - long?

Em
Fa - ther Mc - Ken - zie, writ - ing the words of a ser - mon that no one will hear,
C
Em
no one comes near. Look at him work - ing,
C
darn - ing his socks in the night when there's no - bod - y there,
Em
7fr.
Em7
Em6
Em(♭6)
what does he care? All the lone - ly peo - ple, where do they all come from?
T
A
B

Em
Em7
Em6
Em(♭6)
Em
All the lone - ly peo - ple, where do they all be - long?
C
Em
Ah look at all the lone - ly peo - ple!
C
Em
Ah look at all the lone - ly peo - ple!
Em
El - ea - nor Rig - by, died in the church and was bur - ied a - long with her name,

C
8fr.
Em
7fr.
Em
nobody came.
Father McKenzie,
T
A
B
C
8fr.
wiping the dirt from his hands as he walks from the grave,
Em
7fr.
Em7
Em6
Em(♭6)
no one was saved.
All the lonely people, where do they all come from?
Em
Em7
Em6
Em(♭6)
Em
All the lonely people, where do they all belong?
slower

I'll Cry Instead.

Words & Music by John Lennon & Paul McCartney

I'd get my - self locked up to - day, But I can't
I'd try to make you sad some - how, But I can't,
G7 3fr.
G9 3fr.
D
so I'll cry in - stead.
so I'll cry in - stead.
G7 3fr.
G9 3fr.
1.
2.
I've got a
Don't want to
Bm
A7
cry when there's peo - ple there, I get shy when they start to stare,
T
A
B

D
I'm gon - na hide my - self a - way hey but
B
E
A
D7
I'll come back a - gain some day. And when I
B T
G7
G9
3fr.
do you'd bet - ter hide all the girls,
B T T T
('cause) I'm gon - na break their hearts all 'round the world.
B T T T

D
C7
Yes, I'm gon - na break 'em in two,
I'll show you what your lov - in' man can do, Un - til then
Lay right palm lightly across strings, near bridge, for muffled sound on single note run.
G7
3fr.
D
I'll cry in - stead.
1.
G7
G9
2.
G
Don't want to stead.
T
A
B

Paperback Writer.

Words & Music by John Lennon & Paul McCartney

C/G
want to be a pa - per - back writ - er, pa - per - back
want to be a pa - per - back writ - er, pa - per - back
T
A
B
B
G7
writ - er. It's the dirt - y sto - ry of a dirt - y man, and his
writ - er. If you real - ly like it you can have the rights, it could
T
A
B
B
cling - ing wife does - n't un - der - stand. His son is work - ing for the
make a mil - lion for you o - ver - night. If you must re - turn it you can
T
A
B
B
Dai - ly Mail; It's a stead - y job but he wants to be a pa - per-back
send it here, But I need a break and I want to be a pa - per-back
T
A
B
B

C/G
G7
1.
2.
writ - er, pa - per-back writ - er.
writ - er, pa - per-back writ - er.
T
A
B
B
N.C.
Pa - per - back writ - er,
G7
Repeat and fade
Pa - per - back writ - er.

10/95(22721)